Frederick Peterson

In the Shade of Ygdrasil

Frederick Peterson

In the Shade of Ygdrasil

ISBN/EAN: 9783744651844

Printed in Europe, USA, Canada, Australia, Japan

Cover: Foto ©ninafisch / pixelio.de

More available books at **www.hansebooks.com**

NOTE.

Some of the following verses were published in a volume entitled *Poems and Swedish Translations* in 1883. Others have appeared since then in *Lippincott's Magazine*, the *Cosmopolitan*, the *London Academy*, and other periodicals, and the author must acknowledge his indebtedness to their publishers for the right to reprint them.

NEW YORK, *March, 1893.*

CONTENTS

	PAGE
HEREDITY	1
ENVIRONMENT	3
MICROCOSM	4
THE SWEETEST FLOWER THAT BLOWS	5
SOLITUDE	6
RESURGAM	7
THE IDIOT	8
THE FLAME IN THE WIND	9
THE CRUSADER	10
THE WAYSIDE CRUCIFIX	11
IN THE HARZ	12
VILLANELLE	13
THE SICILIAN TRIAD	15
A STUDY IN GRAY	17
HAPPINESS	18
SORROW	19
CREMATION	20

CONTENTS

	PAGE
In the Rose-Garden of Saadi	22
My Lady Lay All Listlessly	23
A Morning Song	24
To Psyche	25
The Zoroastrian	26
Between the Twilight and the Dawn	27
An Unforgotten Song	29
Solace	30
What Dying Is	31
In Prison	33
The Arrows	34
The Water-Lilies	35
The Robber	37
Snow	38
On the Moldau	39
Foreshadowing	40
A Night Thought	41
Autumn Song	42
A Rainy Night	43
At the Green-Fir Tavern	45
To a Songstress	47
The Sisters	49
Clairvoyance	50
To the Silent King	51

CONTENTS

	PAGE
THE BLIND MAN AND THE SLEEPER	54
THE BLUEBELLS' CHORUS	58
THE NUN	59
REMORSE	60
SPHINX FOUNTAIN	61
VISITATION	62
THE QUEST	63
OFF CRETE	64
WINTER	65
A BALLAD OF WAR-TIME	66
TO LITTLE ROSALIE	68
THE WRAITH AND THE ROSES	70
THE PYTHONESS	71
THE POEM	72
TO AN OUTCAST	73
LENAU	74
THE MUMMY	75
TO LILI	76
HIDE AND SEEK	77
MOONRISE	78
THE PHANTOMS IN MY DREAMS RESEMBLE	79
SAY NOT GOOD-BYE	80
A HEALTH	81
TO A MODERN LILITH	82

CONTENTS

	PAGE
A Wish	83
Steadfastness	84
From the Prison Windows	85
The Lonely House	86
Nature and Man	87
The Unknown Music	88
The Oasis	89
Migration	90
Slumber Song	91
To Count Carl von Snoilsky	92
Where'er You Go	93
An Idle Sparrow's Song	94
Her Soul and Body	95
A Wood Thought	96
Reincarnation	97
Sunset	98
Resignation	99
In a Dahabiah	100
Resurrection	103
Starlight and Bulbul	104
The Dream-Child	105
With Some Lilies-of-the-Valley	106
For a Dead Comedian	107
Fate	108

CONTENTS.

	PAGE
THE LOST ARGOSIES	109
HYPNOTISM	111
HOPES	112
NO MORE	113
WIND-MUSIC	114
DO NOT GROW OLD	116
TWO VIOLETS SHINING IN THE DEW	117
THE CHURCH OF ST. JACQUES	118
RONDEL	119
A SONG OF YESTERDAY	120
EAST AND WEST	121
REMINISCENCE OF TATOI	122
WITH A BOOK OF VERSES	123

IN THE SHADE OF YGDRASIL.

HEREDITY.

I MEET upon the woodland ways
    At morn a lady fair;
Adown her slender shoulders strays
    Her raven hair;

And none who looks into her eyes
    Can fail to feel and know
That in this conscious clay there lies
    Some soul aglow.

But I, who meet her oft about
    The woods in morning song,
I see behind her far stretch out
    A ghostly throng—

A priest, a prince, a lord, a maid,
    Faces of grief and sin,
A high-born lady and a jade,
    A harlequin—

Two lines of ghosts in masquerade,
    Who push her where they will,
As if it were the wind that swayed
    A daffodil.

She sings, she weeps, she smiles, she sighs,
    Looks cruel, sweet or base ;
The features of her fathers rise
    And haunt her face.

As if it were the wind that swayed
    Some stately daffodil,
Upon her face they masquerade
    And work their will.

ENVIRONMENT.

HIGH up around the mountain rock
   Wild sweep the lightning and the storm ;
The spruce grows firm against their shock,
   Stunted and gnarled and rude of form,
With twisted roots that interlock.

But by the rivulet far below,
   Up from the rich dark loam and drift,
Where storms come not and winds are slow,
   Behold the stately willow lift
And sway long branches to and fro !

MICROCOSM.

Upon the morning path one sees,
    When all the land is green and new,
The sun, the skies, the clouds, the trees,
    Deep-mirrored in a drop of dew.

Ah, had we more than mortal eyes
    To pierce the sombre shadows here,
Might we not see how trembling lies
    The universe within a tear?

THE SWEETEST FLOWER THAT BLOWS.

The sweetest flower that blows
  I give you as we part;
For you it is a rose;
  For me it is my heart.

The fragrance it exhales,
  (Ah, if you only knew!)
Which but in dying fails,
  It is my love of you.

The sweetest flower that grows
  I give you as we part;
You think it but a rose;
  Ah, me! it is my heart.

SOLITUDE.

It is the bittern's solemn cry
    Far out upon the lonely moors,
Where steel-gray pools reflect the sky,
    And mists arise in dim contours.

Save this, no murmur on their verge
    Doth stir the stillness of the reeds;
Silent the water-snakes emerge
    From writhing depths of water-weeds.

Through sedge or gorse of that morass
    There shines no light of moon or star;
Only the fen-fires gleam and pass
    Along the low horizon bar.

It is the bittern's solemn cry,
    As if it voiced, with mournful stress,
The strange hereditary sigh
    Of age on age of loneliness.

RESURGAM.

The stars shine clearly in the winter night;
   Beneath the ice no stream is heard to run;
The old green fields are still and waste and white;
   River and field are now become as one.

But not for aye shall all this silence be,
   Erelong new life shall stir beneath the snow,
And we may hear quite softly presently
   The murmur of grasses and the river's flow.

So, O my heart, though thou mayst soon become
   Likewise as cold, and lie as silently,
It is not long that thou must sleep, be dumb,
   Before again new life shall thrill through thee!

THE IDIOT.

Through his misshapen soul and brain
   No thought has passed and left its trace,
And all that brings man joy and pain,
   Finds in his heart no dwelling-place;
     His life is the world's stain.

The horrid vacant visage leers
   And shows its heritage of woe,
Its scars—the sins of ancient years.
   Could any love or hate it?—No!
     Pity may give her tears.

THE FLAME IN THE WIND.

It starts and shivers, pales and trembles,
  Now fixed and certain, now despairing;
Now thin, it some wan ghost resembles,
  Once bright and beaming and uncaring.

At length behold it leap and quiver,
  With its last strength, but fade in trying
Thus I too start and pale and shiver,
  Now fixed and certain and now dying.

THE CRUSADER.

His loved ones from the turret see
   The knight with lance and shining mail
Who rides away across the lea—
   O Heaven forbid that he should fail!

Long years he fights in holy wars
   In the far lands of Palestine,
And now returning with his scars,
   He dreams of those who wait and pine.

Victorious from the Holy Lands,
   He seeks again his native shores;
Red in the sun his castle stands—
   But weeds have grown before his doors!

THE WAYSIDE CRUCIFIX.

A WOODEN Christ, beside the way,
   It marks this still and sacred spot,
Where people passing, pause to pray
   That He forget them not.

The winds are cold and black the skies,
   The rain falls from that drooping face
Like tears, like tears from sorrowing eyes,
   And floods the holy place.

It is a pitying Christ! alas!
   And shall I halt or shall I flee?
O should I pray here as I pass
   That He forget not *me?*

IN THE HARZ.

Across the mountain and the valley
    The goat-bells tinkle, tinkle, tinkle;
The warm winds whisper, sing and dally
    In heather bloom and periwinkle;

The fir-trees change their gloom for smiling;
    The long sounds from the distant churches
Float up enchanting and beguiling,
    And lose themselves among the birches;

The red-roofed hamlets seem like roses
    Which drowsily the eyes may number,
And far and wide the blue sky closes
    O'er those who dream and those who slumber.

VILLANELLE.

Through these long months thy love shall bless
   A lonely roamer over seas,
So love me more and sorrow less.

Each tender smile, each past caress—
   How very dear to him are these,
Whom through long years thy love shall bless,

Who to his bosom aye shall press
   The new-found flower of love—heart's-ease!
So love me more and sorrow less.

To listening Fates each night address
   A low-voiced prayer upon thy knees,
That they long years our love may bless.

Perhaps the pitying Sisters guess
   How Hope the loveless bosom flees :
Love, love me *more*—to sorrow less!

Love shall come back in tenderness,
   Across the months, across the seas,
The steadfast love thy love doth bless ;
So love me more and sorrow less.

THE SICILIAN TRIAD.

Where are they gone,
  Ah, whither fled,
The songs at dawn?
Where are they gone?
We muse upon
  Their singers dead.
Where are they gone,
  Ah, whither fled?

Sweet sounds they drew
  From heath and hill,
Where soft winds blew—
Sweet sounds they drew,
Grown faint and few
  And almost still;
Sweet sounds they drew
  From heath and hill.

Ah, now no more
  Such songs are sung.
The years of yore
Come now no more,
With their sweet lore
  In sweeter tongue.
Ah, now no more
  Such songs are sung.

A STUDY IN GRAY.

The trees are gray, and gray the grasses,
Since autumn flamed and died in glory;
The skies, the seas, the mountain-masses,
    Are gray and hoary.

The light grows gray when evening flashes
Her beams across the tower and spire;
And ah, how gray are now the ashes
    Of love once fire!

HAPPINESS.

She smiles and sings the livelong day—
　A very happy maiden she,
Whose blessed fancies charm away
　Her sorrows and her misery.

How sad and strange the people here!
　They sigh and shriek and whisper things
To shun, to loathe, to dread, to fear—
　But all the day she smiles and sings.

'T is sweet to know that there can be
　Someone whose woe has taken wings—
A very happy creature she
　Who all the day long smiles and sings!

SORROW.

She came a queen in robes of gray,
   And doleful chants her maidens sung;
She drove alas! all joy away,
   With her sad eyes and mournful tongue.

"And art thou really Sorrow?" her
   Some sudden fancy made me ask;
She answered not, but I aver,
   I saw her smile behind her mask!

CREMATION.

Thou tender blossom, more than human,
   Because so fair and pure and humble,
O lovely flower, how could I doom one
   So dear to droop defiled—to crumble
     Like man and woman!

And so, thou flower of flowers, I swore it
   That one thing, one, should not so perish,
That mocking Fate should laugh not o'er it,
   Not alway mar what most I cherish,
     While I deplore it.

Thus on the white hot coals I place thee,
   Among the ferns of some gone æon;
In shining vesture they do grace thee,
   And perfumes as from isles Ægean
     Do soft embrace thee.

No taint, no blemish, naught but ashes—
  Of such fine death thy frame is worthy :
The ermine couch with damask flashes,
  Quick change of heavenly back to earthy,
    No soul abashes.

O bud half-open, thy sweet splendor
  Is risen from the fiery portal,
And atoms which through stem so slender
  Had crept into a bloom immortal,
    Their work surrender !

IN THE ROSE-GARDEN OF SAADI.

A RARE old garden this is, Saadi;
   You made it centuries ago,
   But roses here still bloom and blow,
And souls are called here from the body
   To wander happily to and fro.

A rare old garden, Saadi, this is,
   To walk in when the winds are brusk;
   These flowers exhale an opiate musk
Which soothes the spirit in its blisses
   Afloat upon the purple dusk.

This garden, Saadi, rare and old is:
   Whom can I ask to share its bloom,
   Its damask vapors and perfume,
Its red beds where the sunset's gold is?
   Whom else to share it, Saadi, whom?

MY LADY LAY ALL LISTLESSLY.

My lady lay all listlessly,
With the doomed day about to die;
And did her lips in moving pray?
    'T was thus my lady lay.

Her eyes were full of sombre light,
As if she knew of nearing night
And gazed upon an unknown way—
    'T was thus my lady lay.

Half rising heavily on her hand,
She looked a long look o'er the land
Growing with gloaming into gray—
    Then low my lady lay.

A soft sob and a softer sigh,
Like leaves that stir when winds pass by—
Be meek and mourn as mourn I may,
    For low my lady lay.

A MORNING SONG.

The night is gone, the winds renew,
   The stars have vanished one by one;
The flowers uplift their cups of dew
   And drink a health unto the sun.

The balmy air is full of bloom;
   White drifts are wafted to and fro,
Filling the orchard's ample room
   With soft, sweet-scented summer snow.

I could no longer find my woes
   Were I to seek them all the day;
They are too deep in summer snows,
   The orchard blooms are in the way!

TO PSYCHE.

Blown by the wind and pale as a flower or a phantom,
Lo! thou gleamest again at the gate of the garden,
Which the sun and the moon no longer remember,
    Nor angels keep ward in.

Come, let me once more clasp and hold and behold thee,
Just as of old where the last gleam red in the snows is,
Though there are leaves no longer, though low are the lilies,
    Though ruined the roses.

Stay, I will open the gate of the olden garden,
Wait, thou shalt enter the heart that is worn and shattered,
Whose fair hopes are gone and forever forgotten,
    Like flower-leaves scattered.

Circles of cloud arise on the far horizon,
Gather and cover with gloom the gold of the garden,
Which the sun and the moon no longer remember,
    Nor angels keep ward in.

THE ZOROASTRIAN.

As once perhaps in olden days
    Beneath the far-off Persian skies,
Some reverent one of patient ways
    Did hours before the sun arise,
To hasten in the starlit morn
    Up some high hill when winds were cold,
To wait the moment day is born,
    To kneel before the disk of gold;
And when the long rays were descried,
    Which leaped forth from the golden rim
Of that great star he deified,
    To pour out orisons to him—
As may have done this devotee,
    I wake, I wait, I kneel to *thee!*

BETWEEN THE TWILIGHT AND THE DAWN.

Between the twilight and the dawn,
   While slumber holds my limbs and senses,
Save the slow breathing, life has gone
   And left to sleep her slight defenses.

How still my body lies, how quiet,
   Between the twilight and the dawn!
How much more madly fancies riot
   Because it sleeps in silence on!

How much more wild, how much more free,
   How much more fanciful my soul is!
It roams thy room, unknown to thee,
   Entranced among thy holy holies.

And oh, if it do bend so near
   That thy too tremulous lips it brushes,
Yet in thy dreaming have no fear,
   But sleep on in unbroken hushes!

To some sweet place my soul is gone,
   While slumber holds my limbs and senses,
Between the twilight and the dawn—
   O Death, destroy their frail defenses
And let them moveless slumber on!

AN UNFORGOTTEN SONG.

ONE day to me an angel gave
    A melody unknown of men ;
Down in my heart I made a grave—
    The song I buried then.

I did not make the grave so deep
    In that long gone remembered hour,
But that its ghost now haunts my sleep
    With all its mournful power.

There is a murmuring in my sleep—
    A melody unknown of men—
I did not make its grave so deep
    But that it comes again.

SOLACE.

When ills assail you and Hope shows no way,
   And Beauty dwells apart,
Then shut your eyes against the garish day,
   Look down into your heart!

When sordid cares quench even the soul's light,
   And discord dims and mars,
Go forth into the loneliness of night
   And scan the quiet stars!

WHAT DYING IS.

To leave the turmoil and the careful tumult,
And wander vaguely to a pleasant region
Where green fields glow with sheen of summer sunset,
And narrow farther to a sylvan vista
Whence issue sounds to soothe the spirit's trouble;
To hear the laugh and gurgle of low waters,
And young birds singing with diviner music,
And young birds carolling with lovelier music,
And evening winds that walk with fainter footfall
Unto the white clouds and the bluer sky-depths;
To rest a little some green willow under,
Whose branches whisper in the shadow-garden,
And hold the hand which hath the tenderest pressure,
And touch sweet lips just as thine eyes are closing:
This is that failing ere the sunset's fading,
This is that dying ere the morn immortal.

To see blue-hooded violets reposing
Among the grasses twining to caress thee
And kiss thy cheek, as if thou wert a sister,
And warm thee with their breath of heavenly odor,
As if thou wert to them indeed a sister;
To find some quiet in the willow vista,
Some little slumber in the shadow-garden :
This is that evening of thy dreamless sleeping,
This is that slumber ere the life immortal.

A gentle waking to a newer beauty,
A gradual unfolding to the soul-life,
As 't were a rose's chrysalid transported
Into the blooming valley of that Eden ;
A slow unfolding of an early blossom ;
A little kneeling at the sapphire portals,
And consciousness of all surcease of heartache,
Tumultuous tremor as the soul receiveth
The grander splendor of the spheral chorus
That joy which "passeth human understanding" :
This is that coming of another morning,
This is that morning of the life immortal !

IN PRISON.

Dear maid! put your head to my breast, you will hear
    The prisoner drearily pacing his cell—
What's this! does he stumble, or dream you are near,
    And dreaming you near does he stumble as well?

For twenty long years in the gloom I have heard
    The prisoner's footsteps—for twenty or more—
Life-sentence it is—and he never has stirred
    From his steady, strong tramp till this hour before!

Dear maid! put your head to my breast, you will hear
    The prisoner knock in the gloom of his cell—
How he strikes on the walls, in his frenzy and fear,
    Lest you go and not hear what he wishes to tell!

THE ARROWS.

I am sore wounded ;
I sat in the woodland
  As the moon rose ;
I arose when the moon did,
And walked in the woodland ;
  How sad the wind blows !

She came when the moon did,
The sweet rose, the fair rose ;
  How the wind sighs !
Ah ! I am sore wounded,
By the keen arrows
  That came from her eyes.

THE WATER-LILIES.

On slender piles above the river,
  The mansions of the lakemen stand;
The calm blue waters kiss and quiver;
  The airs bring perfume from the land.

All day the lakemen dreaming lie,
  The fine airs over, waters under,
On golden beds beneath the sky
  Which sunshine makes a golden wonder.

At night-fall close their four green doors
  Lest some stray moonbeam, dangerous fellow,
Should feast upon the precious stores
  Of perfume and of honey mellow.

All night the lakemen lie in slumbers,
  The too sweet day in sleep forgetting;
The waves chime low in tuneful numbers;
  No memory makes a vain regretting.

Happy the lakemen dreaming so
    Upon their couches golden-yellow,
With nought of sorrow or of woe—
    Would I were with them, careless fellow!

THE ROBBER.

Quick! see the lawless brigand go
   Around the hill and through the wold,
With pearls and diamonds all aglow,
   And all agleam with stolen gold!

Now hidden in the secret woods,
   He hath no longer need to fret,
But softly counts his precious goods—
   The robber is the rivulet.

SNOW.

Some snowflakes fallen from afar,
   Pale, cold, of shining purity,
Seem like unto a beauteous star,
   But they are much more like to thee—
I cannot write how like they are.

The sun may look out any day,
   And they will seek again the skies,
But not till melted quite away
   To drops which sparkle like thine eyes-
Ah me, if thou wouldst melt as they!

Because so beautiful and far,
   So pale and cold in purity,
I deem them like a lovely star,
   But they are much more like to thee—
Ah Heaven, how very like they are!

ON THE MOLDAU.

The sun lies red upon the river,
    The last glad sun that we shall see,
For night comes soon to part forever,
    To part forever you and me.

We have known joy, we have known sorrow,
    We have known, ah! too much of pain—
But more and more and more to-morrow
    Shall come the shadows back again.

The sun lies red above the river,
    The last glad sun that we shall see,
For night comes soon to part forever,
    To part forever you and me.

FORESHADOWING.

THY innocent heart it has throbbed into breaking,
And a trance in thy face makes it paler and colder—
How blest is the fancy there may be a waking
    When the ages are older !

That somewhere away in the barren abysses
My shadow may meet thine, and mingle·in meeting
With sweeter caresses than those of our kisses,
    Which on earth were so fleeting !

That mine may afar in strange regions draw near it,
Abroad in the cold, in the dim-lighted spaces ;
That again and again and again the dark spirit
    It may clasp in embraces !

O Fancy, sweet Fancy, steal, steal away reason,
And tell me when comes this divorcement from sorrow,
And when shall this bliss be, this heavenly season—
    To-morrow ? To morrow.

A NIGHT-THOUGHT.

Up from my heart's recesses,
    In dream-wrought draperies,
Thy spirit often presses
    Among my phantasies.

Yet spite of my persuading,
    Erelong thou art away—
No charm can keep thy fading
    Sweet soul till break of day.

Thou comest and thou goest,
    Still, softly, silently;
My heart 's the shrine thou knowest,
    I 'll keep it sweet for thee.

And none shall know thy story
    Until thine eyes renew
The sombre old brown glory
    That gleamed ere they withdrew.

AUTUMN SONG.

Mournfully we gather up the treasures of the meadows,
  Knowing that the winter will destroy the many flowers;
Icy is his breath; he ever broods amid the shadows,
  Where of old the thrushes through the happiest of hours
      Sang among the bowers.

Search no more the woodland's immemorial dream-spaces
  For the golden summer that had scattered her sweet nard in
All the old remembered and most musical of places—
  Lo! behold the Storm-king as he spreads upon the garden
      Snows to drift and harden.

A RAINY NIGHT.

The night is dark and long winds moan;
   Without, the firelight casts no glow;
The rain repeats its undertone
   Unceasingly of woe.

Strange! but it seemed a face looked in,
   So piteously and yet so mild;
Some mother dead it must have been,
   Who seeks her sorrowing child.

"Come to me, grieve no more, ah, stay!
   May I not be beloved too?
I will throw off these robes of clay
   To roam the earth with you."

Then all the window seemed aflame
   From features heavenly, womanly,
"Mother of God, I know thy name—
   Turn not thy face from me."

It is a dream—the long winds moan ;
   Without, the firelight casts no glow ;
The rain repeats its undertone
   Unceasingly of woe.

AT THE GREEN FIR TAVERN.

Down through the windows open wide,
    To fix the noonday on the floor,
The fir-tree's gloomy fingers glide—
    They glide and pause and glide once more.

There sits the round-faced drowsy host!
    Perhaps some phantom from his pipe,
Floats forth to lull—some smoke-like ghost
    Of Bacchus when the grape is ripe.

Without, a gray old harper stands,
    And through the noiseless golden noon,
The strings pour forth beneath his hands
    A wailing, sweet Italian tune.

A lonely traveller sits and dreams,
    And dreams have filled his soul anew:
The mountain wine, the music, seems
    To set his sad heart singing too.

For Her the harper strikes the strings;
  The traveller's dream, this song, is Hers;
And loud of Her the throstle sings
  Within the twilight of the firs.

TO A SONGSTRESS.

A TONE melodious and low
    As we have sometime heard in dreams,
With mellow, modulated flow
    Of murmurs under streams,
A tone blithe birds in happy valley,
    On branches swaying to and fro,
May answer clear and musically.

That tone is thine, and since to me
    It seems as sweet and rare a note
As e'er was plained by bird, or bee
    That singeth in a lily's throat,
Then let my verse faint, far and lowly,
    Breathe these poor praises unto thee,
As echoes of their echoes wholly.

But if thy *voice* be sweet and rare
    As tunes of rill and bird and bee,
Thyself art like the lily fair
    Wherein the bee sings joyfully;
And well do they who feel the power
    Of one dear song of thine declare,
"Yea, thou art like unto a flower!"

THE SISTERS.

O DO you see them, the four who love me,
   The mournful sisters, whose voices hollow
Come floating ever around, above me,
   And call me alway to follow, follow?

Their pale hands beckon, their forms are swaying,
   Like white mist-columns o'er marshy sedges;
O do you see them, the phantoms straying
   Far down and over the world's drear edges?

And one is sister of Sin and Sorrow—
   They call her Madness, her eyes are hollow,
She knows no dying, she knows no morrow;
   And Death another—and " Follow, follow!"
They wail forever around, above me—
O do you see them, the four who love me?

CLAIRVOYANCE.

Deep in your lovely eyes I see
    A wide, mysterious domain ;
Shadows which flicker fitfully
    Around the portals of your brain.

What phantoms hurry to and fro,
    What hidden lights, what sudden gleams,
Down in the catacombs of woe,
    And through the corridor of dreams !

TO THE SILENT KING.

O THOU austere and silent king,
   No more my fancies do forswear thee,
But to thy shadowy shrine they bring
   This token of the love I bear thee.

Though whom thy sad and fatal eyes
   Do fix upon must fail and falter,
Though whom they see—to-morrow dies—
   I hang these verses at thy altar.

I hang them at thy shrine, O king,
   Amidst the moaning and the sighing!
From hate I turn to worshipping,
   And unto loving from defying.

If that God be, as mortals say,
   Who changes what seems sweet to curses,

Then bids us kneel to Him and pray—
   I turn from Him to ask thy mercies.

Or if, as fewer men conceive,
   All soul is due to dust's endeavor
Its lowly form and place to leave—
   How much more am I thine forever!

For after all, to him who fails,
   Whom thy stern eyes so wear and wither,
Thy fatal look so blights and pales,
   Thy influence draws unswerving hither,

Thou grantest this : that he shall sleep
   Through all these centuries' uproar listless,
In earth's great tumult silence keep—
   A sweet oblivion and resistless.

Ah! him thy beauteous eyes shall hold
   Till grief is gone and past is passion ;
Then shalt thou to thy bosom fold
   Him dreamless in thy pitying fashion.

So, Wearer of the Cypress Crown,
   Thou sombre liege of my adoring,
Here at thy feet I lay me down,
   Thy mercy and thy aid imploring :

That thou wilt erelong deign to lay
   Upon my head thy hand forgetful,
So soothing all these shapes away
   Which haunt me in this fever fretful ;

Till care and weariness shall cease
   For me within these shadows kneeling,
And I shall feel thy blissful peace,
   Thy drowsy languor through me stealing ;

And thou shalt hold me with thine eyes,
   No more this bitterness deploring,
Through all these noisy centuries,
   Thou silent God of my adoring !

THE BLIND MAN AND THE SLEEPER.

I DREAMED that I was blind and groping
    Through some strange door,
Knowing not where I was, but hoping
    To fathom more.

My hands had grown so quick to measure,
    My ears to hear—
Though blind I felt a keen sweet pleasure,
    But not a fear.

I thrust aside the silken curtain,
    And entered there,
And roses' fragrance, faint, uncertain,
    Filled all the air.

Upon the floor's thick heavy lining
    I made no sound,

While carven chairs of quaint designing
    I groped around.

Fantastic hangings, figured panels
    And oaken wall,
Old books that haply held strange annals—
    I felt them all.

Sudden I started at a sighing
    And seemed to hear
A light breath as of someone lying
    In slumber near.

The perfume of the rose grew deeper,
    As to and fro
With the soft breathing of the sleeper,
    I felt it flow.

I stood in doubt and hope and wonder
    And called a name,
Half-frightened lest it were a blunder—
    No answer came.

And yet I knew her, I, her lover,
    Who could not see,
And bending down I leaned above her—
    The rose was she.

I felt the sofa's deep recesses,
    The silken gown,
Whereon like one long stream, her tresses
    Went flowing down.

I dared to touch the drooping eyelid,
    The smooth curved cheek,
And fancied that in dreams she smilèd
    And fain would speak.

Though like a reed my soul was shaken
    For love of her,
I said "No word of mine shall waken
    The slumberer."

Again I stood and grasped the curtain
    At the strange door;

The roses' fragrance then uncertain
    Grew more and more.

Ah, I should go and she should never
    Dream that I spoke;
So I passed through forever, ever—
    And then awoke.

Thus must we pass through life, and dying,
    Leave nought divined.
You sleep—how safe from sounds of sighing!—
    And I am blind.

THE BLUEBELLS' CHORUS.

CHANSON FANTASTIQUE.

Our carillon will carol on
   In mellow melody
To invisible dead Isabelle,
   Who is a bell to be,
When the grass grows green upon her grave
   And swallows follow free,
To cling and swing and sing again
   Upon their trysting tree.

Our carillon will carol on
   In firmer murmur then,
When the grass is green as beryl on
   The new grave in the glen,
When invisible dead Isabelle
   Is made a flower again,
To chime and rhyme all time with us
   And know no more of men.

THE NUN.

Hard by a lonely garden walk,
   Too darkly hid for random gaze,
A lily bends upon its stalk,
   And wears a shroud through all its days.

It well might be some holy nun,
   Dead long ago, though living still,
Hidden and pale, bereft of sun,
   And finding life a load of ill.

REMORSE.

I saw you once and in that hour
    I wrote a song to last a day,
Which said your body seemed a flower,
    Your soul its fragrance seemed alway.

You thought me bold; and now I sigh
    Because the sorry rhyme I rue;
Alas! a thoughtless wretch was I
    Who dared compare a flower to *you!*

SPHINX FOUNTAIN.

Long had I sought in crowded cities
   And many a lonely spot
The King of Calm who soothes and pities,
   But found him not.

Till yesterday I reached this valley
   In a dim fragrant wood,
Whither the winds soft-singing rally
   With tones subdued,

Rally around a fountain yonder
   In image of a Sphinx;
Who would have peace with secret wonder
   Stoops down and drinks!

The Sphinx seems heedless of the singing;
   The water bubbles up;
Between its paws is chained and swinging
   A skull for a cup.

VISITATION.

I THOUGHT that I had covered you
   With snows and roses of the years,
That you were dead and never knew
   My face again or felt my tears.

You saw me not, nor felt my tears,
   For you were dead and never knew
How snows and roses of the years
   Had come in drifts to bury you.

But from the grave where you have lain,
   As from the earth some early flower,
You have arisen, my love, again
   To pour forth fragrance hour by hour.

A sad sweet presence hour by hour—
   It is my love has risen again,
As bursts in spring some early flower
   The wintry grave where it has lain.

THE QUEST.

"Where is my body? I cannot find it!
    I have been seeking the wide world over.
O who could hide it, O who could bind it,
    From me a roamer, a lonely rover?
Where is my body? I cannot find it!"

When from the earth-life her soul was parted,
    It stood in silence and woe and wonder,
And now her spirit seeks broken-hearted
    Her body lying the green earth under—
For from her body her soul is parted.

OFF CRETE.

Softly the perfume-giving gales
    Blow from the Cyclades;
They fan the cheeks, they swell the sails,
    They stir the seas.

Above the lovely olive lands
    And waters blue below,
Far up in cloudland Ida stands
    White with white snow.

WINTER.

Now round the rivulet's castle walls
   Resound no more the summer's praises,
But scarce heard through its frozen halls
   A melody runs in secret places:

For though the wood lies deep with snow
   Which veils from us the mosses' slumbers,
The stream with soft, unceasing flow
   Goes gliding down in golden numbers.

What language speaks the beauteous stream,
   With murmurs under its green apsis,
Unconscious voicings of its dream,
   And music of its gentle lapses?

Is this but gravity which sings?
   Or blithe joy in a sense of being,
Or knowledge of more wondrous things,
   And miracles beyond our seeing?

A BALLAD OF WAR-TIME.

At night upon a lonely road
   A traveller hurries fast,
And who has known his drear abode
   Will look at him aghast!

He comes from distant foreign lands,
   And something strange he bears;
He holds his own head in his hands,
   And wofully it stares.

A soldier is he, and was slain
   By some keen scimetar,
And long, long years his form has lain
   By high-walled Temesvar.

Each night his home to find he tries,
   Beside the Elbe wave—
In vain! when dawn is come he lies
   In this same cursèd grave.

Ah, piteous fate, that he who shed
   For love his patriot blood,
Restless and longing, even dead,
   Must lie in hated sod!

At night upon a lonely road
   A traveller hurries fast,
And who has known his drear abode
   Will look at him aghast!

TO LITTLE ROSALIE.

IF you were in my garden, maiden,
    The flowers would say:
"This truly is our little sister
    Of yesterday,
The one we thought the angels laid in
    Her dreams away—
How sweeter, dearer since we missed her!"
    The flowers would say.

They would your tiny form so treasure,
    You could not go,
Your wee, wee feet and hanging tresses
    Entangle so,
That you would lie amidst their pressure
    And sheen and glow
And sweet breath and old-time caresses,
    And could not go.

The trees would look down glad and smiling
    Upon you too ;
The rose-buds would burst quick asunder
    To look at you,
The skies find such blue eyes beguiling
    As lovers do,
And brown bees haunt your mouth in wonder,
    But fear of you.

THE WRAITH AND THE ROSES.

I know a hundred roses
   By their low dreamy names,
And where the wide green close is,
   They rise as rosy flames.

Upon the moonlit hour
   When my beloved returns,
The flame in every flower
   Leaps up and livelier burns.

They wait for her returning,
   For the wraith that wanders round;
And keep their bale-fires burning
   Along the glowing ground.

THE PYTHONESS.

Has none thy grace and beauty sung,
    Nor given thee caresses?
Has no one wish to dwell among
    Thy far off wildernesses?

Yet thou art delicate and fair,
    O fair thou art and slender!
Canst thou not charm into thy lair,
    Nor trust nor love engender?

How bright and strange and strong thine eyes,
    Deceiving and disarming!
'T is good that most of us are wise
    Beyond thy might of harming!

THE POEM.

ALAS! (how sad a word *alas* is!)
   I would again I were that room in,
   So dear because of one dear woman
Whom Memory meets but never passes,
   The chamber her great eyes illumine—
Alas! How sad a word *alas* is!

She was a Poem, a sweet thing created
   By God or some undreamed-of forces,
   Planned ere the suns began their courses,
And in long ages after fated
   To seek again her secret sources—
A gentle Poem, some sweet thing created.

How very sad my soul, alas, is,
   To be again the splendid room in,
   Which those two torches do illumine,
Where Memory halts and never passes,
   Because of love of one dear woman,
But kneels remote in shadowy masses!

TO AN OUTCAST.

In storm and strife,
Amid the city's vicious haunts you grew
Through all your life
Ancestral ghosts made sport of you.

They scoffed, they spurned,
They led where you must stumbling fall;
Where'er you turned,
Fate reared its massive, frowning wall.

LENAU.

You loved the mountain solitude,
  The song of birds, the fragrant air;
And in the silence of the wood
  You felt that God spoke there.

You sang of these in songs so glad
  And holy, that they reached the stars.
Why were you cursed and thus made mad,
  Hemmed in by walls and bars?

THE MUMMY.

I LAID her memory away
   With one sweet rose that she had given,
Here in a secret drawer one day—
   No record has that day in Heaven.

And many soulless years have died
   Ere happy chance again reveals it,
All bandaged, rolled and swathed and tied
   In one long ribbon which conceals it.

Unrolled, but fragrant dust I stir,
   Yet *she* is there as love once showed her—
For the dead rose in its sepulchre
   Embalmed the maiden with its odor.

TO LILI.

Deep in a lonely valley hangs
    A flower so sweet, a flower so pale,
O it were balm for many pangs,
    Could loveliness alone avail!

Its perfumes glide forth on the air
    And fill the wood impalpably;
In sooth, dear maid, the flower seems there
    Not thou—but Earth's late dream of thee!

HIDE AND SEEK.

Though loitering far, I hear the shout
   Of happy children in their play ;
Some hide and others seek them out—
   How sweet it were to be as they !

Ah ! merrily their voices come
   Across the churchyard green to me,
And mingle with the distant hum
   Of wandering wind and bird and bee.

Play, little ones, and run and shout
   Among the purple heather blooms !
If some day cares should be about,
Or old wan Sorrow seek you out—
   Then run and hide among the tombs !

MOONRISE.

At first a luminous red rim
   Rose from the sea behind a sail,
And made it loom up strange and dim,
   A spectre with a gleaming trail.

Then through a cloud all torn in strips
   By winds that wailed above the scars,
Straight through the masts of anchored ships,
   The full moon thrust long golden bars!

THE PHANTOMS IN MY DREAMS RESEMBLE.

The phantoms in my dreams resemble
    The soul of thee;
They tremble as thy soul did tremble
    From love of me;
I fain would clasp them in their tremor
    As I clasped thee,
But frightened fly they from the dreamer,
    Like sounds made free;
Like those sweet sounds the winds are shaking
    From flower and tree,
Which sigh and murmur in awaking
    Melodiously.
Ah, thou dear God, if thou hast power,
    If God thou be,
Restore, restore one gentle hour
    With her to me!

SAY NOT GOOD-BYE.

Say not good-bye, for we shall meet again,
   Perhaps it may be soon—
Somewhere on earth, in sunshine or in rain,
   Beneath the sun or moon.

And if not there, then in some other sphere—
   Perhaps it may be soon—
In some rose-garden where the flowery year
   Keeps always in its June.

Somewhere, somehow, some day—to guess were vai
   Some night or dawn or noon.
Say not good-bye, for we shall meet again—
   Perhaps it may be soon.

A HEALTH.

A STRANGE Knight with his visor drawn,
   With gleaming eye and glancing spear,
Sought entrance at the gate at dawn;
   His princely voice and air austere
   Bespoke both Knight and steed good cheer—
But ere the eve the guest was gone.

Aye, ere the eve came red and brown
   Up from the ocean with the breeze,
The stranger left the coast and town,
   But with the fairest maid of these,
   To cross the gray November seas,
And bind her to his foreign crown.

Deep, deep this bitter cup I drain
   In honor of her gentle eyes,
Her tender mouth that showed no pain,
   Her hair blown under alien skies;
   Of her become the plunderer's prize,
Of her I shall not see again!

TO A MODERN LILITH.

BEHIND your bosom hidden
   Is what you call your heart,
Which sometimes leaps unbidden
   And makes its owner start.

But quiet it, I pray you,
   Lest the coiled secret thing
Should rise up and betray you
   To someone with its sting!

A WISH.

I FAIN would be a troubadour
   (If one poor wish be not a sin)
With voice to charm and song to lure,
   And some melodious mandolin.

Then I would sing a song so sweet,
   So strange and low and strong and brave,
That it should pierce beneath my feet
   And thrill you in your quiet grave!

STEADFASTNESS.

I DO not care what change may come to you
  With the slow passing of your gentle days;
Whether the years molest you and undo
  That outward loveliness, those graceful ways.

No matter if your face and form be marred
  By the vicissitudes of time and dole;
These cannot change the treasures which they gu
  The noble heart, high mind, and generous soul.

FROM THE PRISON WINDOWS.

My soul beholds a lonely lake,
    Around whose sounding shore
A maiden plays upon a lyre
    A melody known no more.

I ask my gaoler if he hears
    Her lyre beneath the stars;
He says it is the wind that beats
    Upon my prison bars.

THE LONELY HOUSE.

Sweet friend she was to one and all,
  More than sweet friend to me.
I sought her door at evenfall
  Just home from oversea.

But at her threshold lay the snow
  In drifts that showed no mark;
The house stood like a thing of woe,
  Empty, deserted, dark.

NATURE AND MAN.

The face of Nature does but rarely change.
    Age after age on everlasting sands
Sing the lone seas their solemn dirge and strange ;
    The rivers run down through the furrowed lands
Held steadfast by the mountains, range on range ;

The summer flowers succeed the winter snows,
    Sunshine the storm, and starry night the day.
Ever returning with the self-same shows
    Insensate matter holds eternal sway,
But conscious soul lives one short hour and goes !

THE UNKNOWN MUSIC.

'T is said in dying one can often hear,
      Ere the soul goes,
Faint melodies that ever come more near,
      But no one knows.

A murmuring, soothing, lulling, lingering sound,
      A holy song,
From the far worlds that we have never found,
      Though seeking long.

Just as the perfume fills a lonely flower
      In the wood's shade,
Ethereal harmonies at the parting hour
      The soul pervade.

It may be echoes of the angels' speech—
      But no one knows—
A far sweet music out of mortal reach,
      Till the soul goes.

THE OASIS.

I CAME from desert solitudes, vast, dreary,
    Mouth parched, and with the glare
Of long gray gleaming levels, eyes grown weary,
    And found sweet solace there.—

A patch of pleasant green, a shady cover,
    A spring, a palm-tree tall ;
And bougainvilleas splashed their crimson over
    A line of yellow wall.

MIGRATION.

Death soon grows busy with the leaves and grass and flowers;
   He brings white cohorts from his frozen Northern caves,
Which shall besiege them in their happy summer bowers,
   And wound and slay and lay them in their whitening graves.

'T is well ye leave the dreary Northern clime and shun
   To meet the icy blasts and snows by winter hurled,
Wise birds, that yearly follow the warm, pleasant sun
   And the green summer, down the sides of the world!

SLUMBER SONG.

Sing a sweet song,
   Tender and low and long,
Until my sorrows deep
   Drowned in the sea of sleep
Never can come again
   With ache or pain.

Over on yonder hill,
   Hear the lone whip-poor-will
Singing in dreams a song—
   Tender and low and long,
Over and over again
   That far sweet strain.

Listen! and then sing slow
   While my heart to and fro
Sways into slumber long
   With the low solemn song,
Never to wake again
   To ache or pain.

TO COUNT CARL VON SNOILSKY.

Rare verse is thine wherein we hear
  The songs of beauty, truth, and art,
And sounding low and deep and clear
  The throbbing of the human heart.

Rare man, in whom harmoniously
  Great thoughts and fancies blend,
Thou art thyself a melody
  Whose music cannot end.

WHERE 'ER YOU GO.

Where'er you go, through sun or shadows,
  Up rocky steeps, or down long hollows,
Across broad moors or flowery meadows,
  Where'er you go, my heart still follows.

To be with you in grief and danger,
  Swifter than is the flight of swallows,
Through Death's domains and regions stranger,
  Where'er you go, my heart still follows.

AN IDLE SPARROW'S SONG.

I AM no travelling tyro
   Nor common stay-at-home,
But have a house in Cairo
   Beyond the midland foam.

'T is in the Sook-Attáreen,
   Where all is life and stir,
Where merchants strange and foreign
   Sell sandal, musk, and myrrh.

As long as winter tarries
   I stay—then seek anew,
Up *via* Rome and Paris,
   My house-boat moored at Kew.

HER SOUL AND BODY.

THE wine was in the golden beaker;
  Its red foam frothed and bubbled up;
For some fine spirit I was seeker;
  I found one in that shining cup.

I longed to breathe the sweets it scattered,
  To breathe, to taste, did Fate permit,
But from my lips the cup fell shattered;
  Then fell and broke my heart with it.

A WOOD-THOUGHT.

THE very stillness weighs upon the ear,
   The very loneliness o'ercrowds the mind,
   As if a thousand shadowy, undefined,
Portentous mysteries were thronging here.

One feels a Presence it were vain to seek,
   Full of all secrets since the world was young;
   And prophecies that tremble on its tongue,
But are unspoken, for it cannot speak.

REINCARNATION.

ONE of your ancestry was likewise fair
    As some soft spring-flower hidden in the snow;
Like yours her eyes were, and her mouth, her hair—
    It is not strange that she was loth to go!

She would not go; more strong her spirit grew,
    Till she might enter your sweet soul's domain,
And work her will there as if *she* were you,
    And smile and charm and bless the world again!

SUNSET.

Leaf after leaf unfolding slowly,
   The sunset blossoms in red and gold,
Tremulous, solemn, peaceful, holy,
   Petal by petal and fold on fold.

First the pink bud and then the flower,
   Leaf after leaf and fold on fold,
Expanding and blending to bloom in an hour
   With rose-colored petals and heart of gold.

But soon the flower is rent and riven,
   The great gold heart droops lower and lower
The petals are scattered in drifts and driven
   Into the night to be seen no more.

RESIGNATION.

All things change and go
  Like the wind and the dew,
Staying a moment so,
  Then hastening anew—
All things change and go;
  Why should not you?
They fade, they fly, they flow;
  Now life goes too.

Now happy life goes too,
  Out into nothingness;
Unseen it passes through
  The portals of distress.
Now happy life goes too—
  Resignedly? Yes.
Wherefore regret or rue
  What could not bless?

IN A DAHABIAH.

A DESERT lies on either hand
   In stern and lone repose ;
Between the wastes of yellow sand
   The dark Nile flows.

All through the valley strait and green
   Are wafted faint perfumes
From fields of clover and sweet-bean
   And lentil-blooms.

Palm groves and minarets and towers,
   Like dreams before the eye,
Pass slowly as through drowsy hours
   Our boat drifts by.

The dark-robed women file in troops
   To fill their water jars,

Where wind-bound boats lie moored in groups
  With idle spars.

All day a strident monotone
  Along the shore line steals—
The noise of wells, the creak and groan
  Of water-wheels.

Out on the river softly floats
  The boatmen's wailing song,
Where up and down the swan-winged boats
  Glide all day long.

Soon sharp against the reddening sky,
  By sunset canopied,
Looms up remote and shadowy
  A pyramid.

Strange sounds by curious wading-birds
  Are heard along the bars,
When night brings forth too fair for words
  Her moon and stars.

Then lo, a ghost !—Seneferoo
　　Comes from his giant tomb
To guard his Egypt all night through
　　On huge Maydoom !

RESURRECTION.

In their sweet graves the violets repine,
    Among the roots of the old sycamore.
When will the snow go and the spring sun shine,
    And there be knocking at their tomb's low door?

Ah, when the gentle angel of the rain
    Shall sound soft summons on each sepulchre,
They will burst straightway from their graves again
    Into God's presence and then scarcely stir!

STARLIGHT AND BULBUL.

Sweetheart so sweet, there is no word
   Can quite portray you as you are,
No form of speech—just song of bird
   And tender light of summer star.

I would that I were very wise,
   That I might tell you what they say
From lonely wood and tranquil skies—
   The star by night, the bird by day.

THE DREAM-CHILD.

How, having held her perfect face
   Between my hands and kissed her mouth,
How could I lose her into space
   Somewhere East, West, or North, or South?

Now sometimes in the crowded street,
   Above the tumult of the throng,
I see, I hear, afar and sweet,
   A phantom face, a haunting song.

Once when the sea was very gray,
   All gray with mist and gray with rain,
I saw her flash and fade away
   In foamy wastes of waves again.

And once in desert lands, I sought
   For peace that has its dwelling there,
When lo! some strange mirage had wrought
   Her face upon the empty air!

WITH SOME LILIES-OF-THE-VALLEY.

This morn awaking in affright,
   They saw the snow instead of May,
Around—the wide land clothed in white ;
   Above—the skies all strange and gray.

And here they are upon their stem ;
   I bring the poor pale things to you
Who will be summer unto them—
   Summer and sun and wind and dew !

FOR A DEAD COMEDIAN.

PLAY no sad air upon the chalumeau,
　　No mournful melody upon the lute,
But rather let the merriest music flow
　　　Up through the chamber where he lieth mute—
　　　　Perhaps he listeneth !

Come then with song and dance and joyful tune !
　　Bring in the cymbals and the stirring fife,
The hautboy and the comical bassoon—
　　　For he who roused up laughter all his life
　　　　Should make a jest of Death !

FATE.

"What must be must be"—say it over and over,
    Until you see and feel its meaning clear,
Till griefs and sorrows that around you hover
    Shall bring no more a tear.

Through all the day repeat it over and over,
    In night and silence, on the land and sea;
Perhaps it will requite you, O world-rover—
    It is philosophy!

Thus bitter balsam does the soul discover
    For life and death and every pain and smart—
A hopeless solace for each mourning lover—
    A balm to ease the heart.

THE LOST ARGOSIES.

I 've looked in vain and long for them,
  My red-sailed galleys and triremes
That sailed a sea too strong for them
  'Mid windy paths and ocean streams,
And now I make a song for them—
    My far-tossed wrecks of dreams.

They sailed and dear shapes went with them
  Swaying along their rosy wales,
And comely rowers sent with them
  Made songs that echoed on their trails;
Sang melodies, and blent with them
    Were sounds of oars and sails.

An island—sirens sing of it—
  They sought with sail and helping oar.

No token yet they bring of it,
   Nor of the careless friends they bore,
Though I am lawful King of it—
   The Isle of Nevermore.

I 've looked in vain and long for them,
   My red-sailed galleys and triremes,
That braved a sea too strong for them
   'Mid windy paths and ocean streams,
And now I make a song for them—
     My far-tossed wrecks of dreams.

HYPNOTISM.

Come nearer, let me see your face,
   For just a moment's space ;
Bend close with those clear tranquil eyes,
   Mysterious, wonder-wise.

Then let your words of magic art
   Like music seek my heart—
"Sleep long—sleep well, whate'er befall,
   Until you hear me call!"—

Then shall sweet visions take control
   Of my blest, happy soul ;
And what if thus—unmoved by fears—
   I sleep a hundred years !

What matter if they bury me
   Deep down in earth or sea !—
I must awaken and rejoice
   When next I hear your voice.

HOPES.

'T is when the spirit is most sorely pressed
   By the long weariness of lonely hours,
New hopes spring up and blossom in the breast,
   Like to a rosebush with a thousand flowers.

They bud, they blossom, then their petals fall
   In downy drifts blown to and fro by sighs—
Disturb them not, for ah, beneath them all
   Perhaps the heart now deeply buried lies!

NO MORE.

A SHADOW creepeth through the door
   With dread to all who hear it,
So softly through the open door,
   With loitering step along the floor,
A shadow with the name *No More*,
   A dim and haunting spirit.

It stirreth in the lonely air
   That breatheth in the hallway;
It rustleth up and down the stair,
   And round the cradle and the chair,
All through the rooms so darkly bare
   It sigheth, sigheth alway.

It lingereth like a faint perfume
   In each uncertain corner;
It stayeth as a still perfume
   Upon the air in every room—
"No more—no more—no more"—the doom
   It murmureth to the mourner!

WIND-MUSIC.

O WIND, the wintry prairie grass
   Sighs and sobs unceasingly,
Rustles and crackles as you pass—
   A wide brown melancholy sea!

Sometimes from out the Northern firs
   Your threnody majestic flows,
And deep the mighty forest stirs
   To sing its centuries of woes.

Or some South garden's loveliness
   Lures you, when violet dusk begins,
To murmur through the fragrances
   Of roses and of mandarins.

And always on the ocean shore
   In a pæan wild or requiem long,

A wailing dirge for evermore,
    One hears your everlasting song.

But what strange joy, what keen delight,
    Are yours, O waif of many lands,
When secretly you find by night
    A wind-harp strung by human hands!

DO NOT GROW OLD.

Do not grow old, there is too much to lose;
   The world has need of all these precious things—
   This fresh young face, these eyes like woodland springs,
This shadowy hair which every zephyr woos,

These subtle graces, all these lovely hues,
   This voice like echoes from melodious strings.
Do not grow old, there is too much to lose;
   The world has need of all these precious things.

Let us not think of blight and frosty dews
   Such as to flowers the harsher season brings,
   But through your body, by sweet chastenings,
Let heart and soul perennial youth diffuse :
Do not grow old, there is too much to lose.

TWO VIOLETS SHINING IN THE DEW.

Two violets shining in the dew
   Look up like eyes at me—I start,
A keen swift memory of you
   Cuts straight into my heart!

For with my soul's eyes I can trace
   A shape that will not let me stir,
With fold on fold of filmy lace
   And shadowy silk and minever.

I see them from a mist of tears!
   Your eyes so tranquil, soft, and blue
Peer through the mould of many years—
   Two violets shining in the dew.

THE CHURCH OF ST. JACQUES.

There is a hush of peace within,
  And in the holy silence there,
A priest says mass for souls of sin;
  And two lone figures kneel in prayer
    Close to the chancel-step.

Outside a ribald throng, a crowd,
  Is loitering round the sacred walls;
They gamble, dance, sing, bawl aloud,
  In tents and booths and market-stalls—
    'T is Sunday in Dieppe!

RONDEL.

A LITTLE love a little while,
   And then we part to meet no more;
   For never can old Time restore
One little sigh, one little smile.

Before us shall the years defile
   A woful line, a phantom corps;
A little love a little while,
   And then we part to meet no more.

Yet ere we come to reconcile
   Ourselves to destiny—before
   We gaze alone from either shore
At the waste waters mile on mile—
A little love a little while.

A SONG OF YESTERDAY.

Come, sweet, and sing these songs again;
　　They made a murmur in my heart,
An echoing sense of loss or pain,
An immemorial soft refrain,
　　So sweet they were, so sweet thou art!

And if upon the morning road
　　I falter weary, lone, and pale,
Some sudden echo lifts the load,
Some strain of yesternight, when flowed
　　The music of the nightingale.

EAST AND WEST.

Shut in with books and pipe and crackling fire,
    Hafiz, I roam with you
A gorgeous garden to my heart's desire!
The bulbul sings as though it might expire
    In balsam, moonlight, dew.

Outside my window-square, the black clouds lower;
    Hear the wind howl and blow!
The shutter creaks; the great trees quiver and cower,
And round yon huge and lonely lantern-tower
    Wild sweeps the wintry snow!

REMINISCENCE OF TATOI.

Sometimes the heart must feed on memories,
   To stay its longings and assuage its pain ;
   Old scenes, old songs, old faces come again,
Else might it perish where no Beauty is,
For life has need of Beauty's ministries.

Thus at this moment all my cares are gone ;
   The hot streets vanish with their wild uproar ;
   I smell the pine-woods and the flowers once more,
And see the sun shine softly down upon
Blue Salamis and gray Pentelikon.

WITH A BOOK OF VERSES.

I would that some one verse of mine
　　Might hold enough of you
To keep it fresh and fair and fine
　　A year or two—

A year or two beyond our death—
　　Surely that were not long
To have your spirit like a breath
　　Pervade my song.

So when one came to turn the leaf
　　Whereon it printed lies,
A perfume keen and sweet and brief
　　Might chance to rise,

As if your lingering soul forsook
　　Some far world here to stay,
As if close shut within the book
　　A crushed rose lay.

www.ingramcontent.com/pod-product-compliance
Lightning Source LLC
Chambersburg PA
CBHW031335160426
43196CB00007B/699